BODACIOUS

Appliqué

à La Carte

MARGIE ENGEL

American Quilter's Society
P. O. Box 3290 • Paducah, KY 42002-3290
www.AmericanQuilter.com

Located in Paducah, Kentucky, the American Quilter's Society (AQS) is dedicated to promoting the accomplishments of today's quilters. Through its publications and events, AQS strives to honor today's quiltmakers and their work and to inspire future creativity and innovation in quiltmaking.

Text © 2008, Author, Margie Engel
Artwork © 2008, American Quilter's Society

EXECUTIVE EDITOR: ANDI MILAM REYNOLDS
GRAPHIC DESIGN: ELAINE WILSON
COVER DESIGN: MICHAEL BUCKINGHAM
QUILT PHOTOGRAPHY: CHARLES R. LYNCH
HOW-TO-PHOTOGRAPHY: JOHN ENGEL

American Quilter's Society
P. O. Box 3290 • Paducah, KY 42002-3290
www.AmericanQuilter.com

Additional copies of this book may be ordered from the American Quilter's Society, PO Box 3290, Paducah, KY 42002-3290, or online at www.AmericanQuilter.com.

Library of Congress Cataloging-in-Publication Data

Engel, Margie.
  Bodacious appliqué à la carte / by Margie Engel.
     p. cm.
  ISBN 978-1-57432-962-9
  1. Appliqué--Patterns. 2. Machine appliqué--Patterns. I. Title.

TT779.E56 2008
746.44'5041--dc22

2008034479

Proudly printed and bound in the United States of America

Grateful Thanks!

To God, *for our creative spirits*

To my family, *for sharing and understanding my passion for fabrics and quilts*

To John Engel, *husband extraordinaire and photographer, for constant encouragement, technical know-how, and never minding the loose threads on his clothing*

To Joan Sheppard, *treasured sister, for warm assistance, a listening ear, and for introducing me to quilts*

To Louise Repath, *trusted friend, for enthusiastic support and practical suggestions*

To my quilting friends, *amazing individuals, for sharing yourselves with me and for being EduQuilters' shining stars*

To my students, *exuberant and inspirational, for your ever-ready spirit of adventure*

To Andi Reynolds, *gifted word masseuse, for being a truly wonderful editor*

Contents! *for Bodacious Appliqué*

Eureka! *Appliqué Meets Interfacing and Colored Pencils*

(Or, How This Book Came About and Where It Is Going)

Glossary

Adhesive is the sticky substance used to make fusible products.

Fusible is a product that has an applied adhesive that allows it (the fusible product) to be melted/fused to another fiber.

Stabilizer is a product that strengthens fabrics to which it is attached, thereby preventing distortion and shifting.

Interfacings are woven or synthetic products used between two or more fabrics to provide stability.

Fusible Web is a thin synthetic web to which an adhesive has been applied that is activated when ironed, preferably between two pieces of fabric.

While on my sewing journey from the garment world, where appliqués had to have turned, soft edges and be stitched invisibly into position, to the quilting world, I found myself moving from simple, unadorned appliqués into another raw-edged, embellished appliqué universe.

With this shift to highly embellished appliqués came a new problem—that of the dreadful, unwanted pucker!

It is a basic fact that when stitch density varies from one place in the fabric to another, puckering is likely to occur. When I examined my densely stitched appliqués, I discovered that it was not the appliqué that was puckered. It was the background puckering around the appliqué because it wasn't as densely stitched.

It became essential that I find a technique that would welcome dense stitching without puckers so that I could produce knockout, bodacious appliqués that would lie flat.

OPPOSITE: *BEAUREGARD (the macaw, up close and personal).*

The solution became clear—create a completed appliqué, stitching to my heart's content, before sewing the applique to its background.

Meanwhile, give the appliqué enough stability to withstand dense stitching by using a fusible interfacing. Fusible interfacing has an adhesive applied on just one side of the fabric. After it is adhered to the wrong side of the appliqué fabric, the exposed side of the interfacing is not sticky. It adds body to the appliqué fabric, and the result feels like one piece of fabric. It also protects the edge of the fabric as does paper-backed fusible web.

There are many fusible interfacings on the market. The trick is to find the correct weight and feel for your project. For embellishing with thread, interfacing on which the adhesive is evenly applied yields better results than those on which the adhesive is applied in dots. The fused fabric is smoother, a necessity for using markers and pencils. My favorite fusible interfacing is 100 percent cotton "Form Flex" produced by HTCW, Inc.

Sometimes, stitch embellishment is so enthralling and dense that it would benefit from a second stabilizer. Stabilizers come in all forms from tearaway to meltaway to washaway. Because I find that tearaway stabilizers compromise the integrity of stitches, I prefer to use a washaway. Sulky® Paper Solvy™ stabilizer serves well as a second stabilizer when needed. I rinse it off by holding it under running water from the tap. If any remains, it does not damage the fabric or alter the feel of the appliqué.

Voilà—pucker problem solved!! Also, creating appliqués a la carte allows you to audition background fabrics that best suit your bodacious creation. Ohmygoodnessgracious, you can try out all your fabrics and change your mind as many times as you wish!

Along this embellished appliqué journey, I began using colored pencils and markers to enhance simple appliqués before stitch embellishing. The first time I used them was for the practical reason of establishing contour lines on a very large, thirty-six inch flower to guide my stitches. Then I added some shading and accent lines. The results were so easily accomplished that I never put the pencils away and added the use of fabric markers for stronger lines.

Occasionally, someone asks why I use colored pencils. The answer is because it is effective and easy. When I teach embellished appliqué classes, students do not fear "messing up" with a colored pencil, whereas they often shy away from picking up a paintbrush. You will find detailed instructions in Step 5, pages 25–32.

Once your appliqué is stitch-embellished and colored to your satisfaction, sew it into position, and you, the appliqué queen, can still embellish a bit more. You can even add a bead or two or a dozen! These appliqués aren't finished until the queen says so!

OPPOSITE: *BEAUREGARD (detail)*

Voilà! *Using the à la Carte Approach*

(Or, In the Time It Takes You to Read This Book, You Can Create a Bodacious Appliqué)

Step 1: Visualize Your Quilt

With a huge variety of tools and materials available, we quilters might be the most blessed people on the planet! Fabrics, tools, and methods exist to suit every personality, every need, and even every whim.

Just how does one select a particular method for a specific appliqué?

The answer lies within your expectations. How do you see the finished project? Visualizing your quilt will provide immediate direction. *Rely on your intuition and your mental picture.* Begin with the method which best fits your idea. Try it out to see if the results are what you anticipated.

Another consideration is how much time and effort you wish to expend on this project. Generally, quilters who select appliqué projects are not primarily concerned with the time spent on a project. Most quilts made in a weekend don't involve much appliqué. We all seem to be painfully aware that time is moving on, so its judicious use must be a consideration.

OPPOSITE: *Detail from* OUT OF THE SWAMP.

Because my goal is to achieve beautiful, well-stitched appliqués in this century, all my appliqués are machine sewn and predominately machine-stitch enhanced until I reach the beading stage. I love stitching on my machine every bit as much as I enjoy hand sewing—a good thing because I also enjoy machine quilting. This means I can get my quilts completed before I am consumed by a new project.

Now it is your turn to visualize your quilt and to move forward. Just for fun, begin with the first appliqué method, "Creating an Illusion of Depth." Do understand, though, that within any single quilt, there is usually reason to use more than one technique. That is why you find four methods within pages 14–20.

Keep one question at the forefront: "What would happen if I changed this or added that?" *Appliqués invite creativity and you will enjoy making them more and more each time you inject yourself, your ideas, and your expectations into their production.*

Step 2: Prepare Your Fabric

In the following pages, the first two appliqué methods use fusible interfacing. Here are the fabric preparation steps for these methods:

Wash the fabric.

⁘ Rinse your fabric, or actually wash it with your favorite soap or detergent. I rinse my fabrics in very hot water, hotter than will ever be used to launder any quilt. This way I know it will be receptive to markers and colored pencils. Additionally, excess dye is gone, and the fabric is preshrunk. Prewashing dark colors is an absolute must for me, since I do not want to experience later the anguish of having them bleed onto lighter fabrics—the price for skipping this step. *Do not use fabric softeners or detergents that include fabric softeners in their compounds.* These elements compromise the fabric's ability to retain fusible webs and/or interfacing.

Prewashing fabrics can avoid later problems.

⁘ Dry the fabric until slightly damp, then iron the fabric dry.

Cut the fabric and fusible interfacing.

⁘ Measure the appliqué design and cut your fabric slightly larger than the measurement.

⁘ Cut a piece of fusible interfacing just slightly smaller than the fabric.

Press the interfacing.

⁘ Place the fabric wrong-side up on the ironing board and iron it well.

⁘ Place the interfacing with the fusible side down onto the fabric. The fusible side (the adhesive) is usually shiny.

⁘ Lightly spray the interfacing with water. Using a steam iron, hold the iron slightly above the interfacing for a few seconds and allow the steam to penetrate it. This preshrinks the interfacing. Begin pressing with an up-and-down motion in the center of the design, continuing outward. There is no time limit to this step. Make sure the interfacing is well attached without wrinkles or bubbles.

⁘ Flip the piece over and repeat the ironing.

⁘ If there are any wrinkles or bumps on the front, now is the time to get them out, while the interfacing is warm and slightly damp and can be manipulated, and even pulled up and pressed a second time if need be.

Your interfaced fabric is now ready for Method One or Method Two. Methods Three and Four do not use interfacing. You may choose to prewash your fabrics, however.

Step 3: Choose a Bodacious Appliqué Method (or Two)

Appliqué can be easy, simple fun, or it can be incredibly involved. Have you ever examined appliqués that were assembled using many, many small pieces of fabric? If you thought that it was pretty but looked too intricate, then consider making appliqués from fewer fabrics and enhancing them with colored pencils, fabric markers, and machine stitches.

The first bodacious appliqué method, **Creating an Illusion of Depth in Appliqué,** is very simple, involving only the use of one or two pieces of fabric and colored pencils and/or thread embellishment to define, shade, and contour.

The second method, **Jigsaw Appliqué Using Multiple Fabrics,** is for large appliqués comprised of several parts. Imagine a flower with five petals for which you want to use different fabrics and values. The jigsaw plan includes step-by-step instructions for achieving this kind of appliqué. Freezer paper facilitates the process.

The unique attribute of these two methods is that you create a one-piece appliqué before cutting it out. *This means that the edges are not vulnerable while you are grasping the fabric to apply embellishments.* All the machine stitching within the appliqué is sewn before you cut it out. This enables you to stitch the appliqué onto its background fabric without puckers.

The occasional moment arises in appliqué creation when using a paper-backed fusible web is both convenient and expedient for completing a design. It may be the addition of some small detail which, though it is needed, does not require much embellishing. This is a great time to draw a mirror image of the detail onto the adhesive's paper backing and then press it into position. Detailed directions are given on page 18 for this third method, **Bonded Appliqué Using Paper-backed Fusible Web.**

Another advantageous use of paper-backed fusible web is to place it between two fabrics, with the wrong sides of the fabrics next to the adhesive. This yields a double appliqué, which lends itself to intricate cut edges. The appliqué is subsequently fastened in methods other than edge stitching. Dandelion leaves, palm trees, and feathers are good examples. Such objects can even be cut freehand if you feel creatively adventurous. You must try this method, if only because it is fun and freeing. See **Double-sided, 3-D Appliqué Using Fusible Web,** Method Four.

Pressing vs. Ironing

Pressing uses an up-and-down motion of the iron. *Ironing* uses a sliding-across-the-fabric motion. Pressing is the best technique for initially applying fusible interfacing to fabric or to fuse appliqué pieces to each other or to the background. Ironing may shift or distort appliqués or fusible interfacings, but it is good for eliminating wrinkles in background fabrics and "finishing" the piece once appliques are firmly in place.

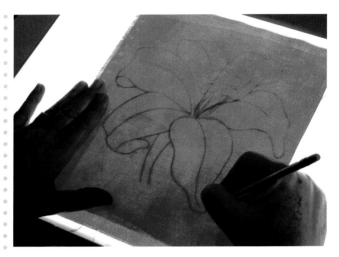

Trace your design directly on the fabric.

Color shadings, contours, and details are created with colored pencils.

Cut out the appliqué after the decorative stitching is finished.

METHOD ONE:
Creating an Illusion of Depth in Appliqué

Use this method for simple designs of one or two fabric pieces and when anticipating a large amount of machine-stitched embellishment in one area.

Detailed Instructions

⁘ Fuse the interfacing to the appliqué fabric, as described in **Step 2, Prepare Your Fabric,** page 12.

⁘ Trace the design directly onto the fabric. Create depth with colored pencils. Refer to the detailed steps in "Hand Coloring on Fabric" in **Step 4, Embellish with Colored Pencils,** page 21.

⁘ Place water-soluble or tearaway stabilizer behind the appliqué, pinning it in the corners.

Enhance with machine stitches as detailed in "Free Motion Embellishing" in **Step 5, Embellish with Thread,** page 31.

⁘ Remove the stabilizer. Give the piece its final pressing. If desired, add more color with pencils or markers.

⁘ Audition the appliqué on the background. See **Step 6, Audition Fabric Background and Stitch,** page 33.

⁘ Cut out the appliqué using your sharpest scissors and stitch it to the background.

⁘ Stand back and admire your work.

METHOD TWO:

Jigsaw Appliqué Using Multiple Fabrics

Some designs leap off the page, crying out to use several fabrics. Large florals, bright, stylized flowers, and birds of many colors are examples. The jigsaw approach answers that call. Approach this method as if the appliqué were a puzzle for which you decide how many pieces to use.

Since the reason for using this method is to incorporate a variety of fabrics into the appliqué, *select sturdy fabrics* and leave the lighter weights for other projects. Batiks work very well.

Creating jigsaw appliqué pattern pieces is simple. First, you have to figure out how many pieces you want. For example, you may wish to make a flower from three different fabrics. In this instance, a design section could be one petal or a grouping of petals. There is no need to draw mirror images. For this method, you work with the design facing upward and produce a composite appliqué which will accept intensive machine stitching.

Detailed Instructions

✤ Study the design. Determine which elements will be separate pattern pieces.

✤ Trace the design onto the dull side of freezer paper. Place the freezer paper shiny side down onto the appliqué pattern. Using a #2 pencil or permanent marker, trace each portion that will use a separate fabric. Label each part. Leave a space between each portion for cutting ease. Cut out the pattern beyond the lines, keeping a small margin.

✤ Select the fused fabric for each jigsaw piece. (See **Step 2, Prepare Your Fabric,** page 12.) Preheat the iron to the temperature appropriate for the fabric. Place the fabric right side up on the ironing board and press it well.

✤ Situate the freezer-paper pattern atop the fabric by turning the appliqué design at an angle so that its longest edges run with the bias grain of the fabric.

✤ Press the freezer paper to the fabric. Allow the piece to cool, then cut the fabric and freezer paper simultaneously on the drawn lines, leaving the freezer paper intact on the fabric.

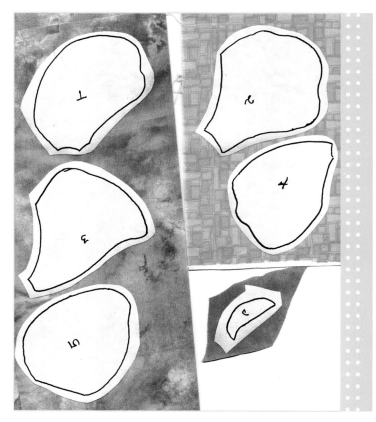

Iron the freezer-paper pattern pieces to the right sides of your fabrics.

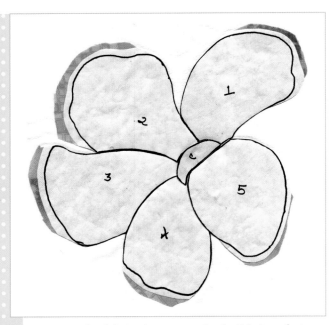

Position the fabric pieces atop the fusible interfacing.

Remove the freezer paper and finish pressing your appliqué.

❖ Cut a piece of fusible interfacing to accommodate the entire motif. Place this on your ironing surface with the fusible side facing upward. Position each appliqué piece, with the freezer paper still on the fabric, atop the adhesive, right-side up. Push each piece directly next to one another. The fabrics sit adjacent, and none overlap, like an assembled jigsaw puzzle.

❖ Once the design is assembled with all the freezer paper touching, cover everything with a pressing sheet. "Heat baste" this assemblage with a dry iron by pressing the center of the piece with an up and down motion to activate the fusible interfacing just enough to grab the fabric. *Do not iron back and forth.* Gently pull off the freezer paper and complete the pressing.

❖ Turn the layers over, keeping the pressing sheet underneath the appliqué. Lightly spray the interfacing with water. Set the temperature on a steam iron to match the appliqué fabric. Beginning in the center, hold the iron a little above the surface and let the steam penetrate the interfacing for a few seconds. Press the entire piece very well, ensuring that the interfacing has completely adhered to the fabric.

❖ Turn the appliqué right-side up and check for bubbles. While warm, the fabric and fusible can still be manipulated.

❖ The appliqué is ready for hand coloring and stitching. Refer to **Steps 4, Techniques with Colored Pencils,** page 23, and **5, Embellish with Thread,** page 25.

METHOD THREE:
Bonded Appliqué Using Paper-backed Fusible Web

When learning to use paper-backed fusible webs, realize that there is a knack to handling them. It may take a moment of patience at the outset, but do not let this daunt you. These products have a definite place and purpose in the quilt world. If you bring them into your sewing room, they may come to number among your best friends.

Paper-backed fusible webs can be purchased by the yard or in packages. They come in various weights, and one variety, Steam-a-Seam2®, comes with two sheets of paper with the adhesive between. The version with paper on each side of the fusible is quite handy when you wish to play with positioning details. This allows you to reposition the fabric several times, giving opportunity to experiment. Once you are pleased with your arrangement, you then press the items permanently with an iron.

Opinions vary from quilter to quilter as to which weight should be used for any given project. Try different weights and brands to see what you prefer, and vary their use according to your project. The heavier the fusible, the stiffer your appliqué. For example, if you want a 3-D leaf (Method Four) to really stand up off the background, you would not choose a lightweight product.

The first step in Method Three is to draw the design onto the paper backing. *Because the adhesive is always placed on the wrong side of the fabric, the drawing must be a mirror image unless the design is the same on each side, such as a heart or other symmetrically shaped motif.*

The second step is to actually *read and follow the manufacturer's instructions.* Amazing, is it not, how often we skip that little detail! Various types of fusible interfacings require different iron temperatures. Some require steam for permanent adhesion; others do not.

Additionally, some adhesives may not adhere to fabrics which have been rinsed in fabric softener. You would be wise to make a habit of using a no-stick pressing sheet or parchment (baking) paper to preserve both the ironing surface and the iron. Protect both by pressing the fabric and fusible interfacing sandwiched between layers of pressing sheets. (Find parchment paper in the grocery store baking aisle.)

Detail from ELEGANTÈ *(bonded appliqué project).*

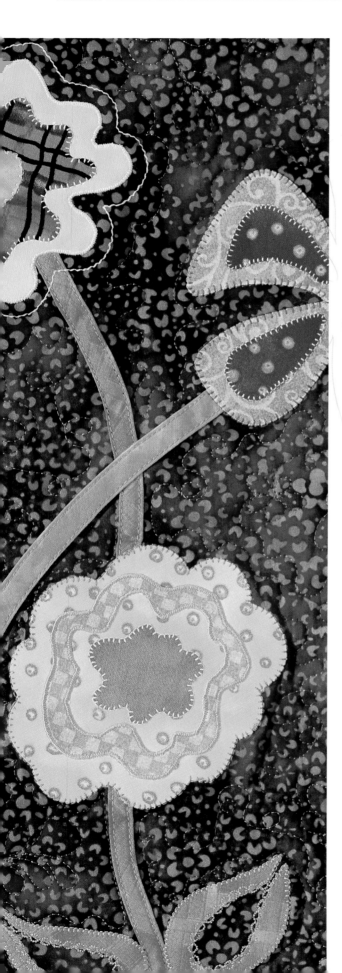

Detailed Instructions

❖ Draw a mirror image of the design onto the paper backing while it is still attached to the fusible web. A #2 pencil works well. Ballpoint pens tend to smear.

❖ Roughly cut out the design, leaving a margin around the pencil drawing.

Note: For the step below, If using a fusible web sandwiched between two papers, first remove the paper which does NOT have the drawing on it.

❖ Place the fusible web, with the drawing on the paper facing up, next to the wrong side of the fabric and press.

❖ Cut out the design on the drawn lines. Use sharp scissors to avoid ragged edges.

❖ Place the appliqué onto its background as desired and press it permanently.

❖ Let the appliqué cool, then remove the paper.

❖ Stitch the appliqué as desired. Refer to **Embellish with Thread, Step 5,** page 25.

LEFT: *Detail from DC's GARDEN OF GLEE (bonded appliqué project).*

OPPOSITE: *Double-sided appliqué dandelion leaves from WINDBLOWN WISHES quilt.*

METHOD FOUR:
Double-sided, 3-D Appliqué Using Fusible Web

Creative delights are yours when you use double appliqués because concerns about sewing down the edges can be abandoned. Flowers, leaves, palm fronds, fish, and just about any item can benefit from this technique. The biggest advantage is that you can stitch them into position through the motif center, allowing the edges to be free and become 3-D.

This is a simple way to add texture to any project, whether the items lie flat or curl up. In this book, they are a necessity for dandelion leaves. Consider double-sided appliqués as viable options for adding leaves or feathers in any project.

Sticky Tip

Appliqué enthusiasts are sometimes unhappy when the adhesive from paper-backed fusible web sticks to the machine needle. The manufacturers tell us that if we follow the instructions, we should not have "goop" on the needle. Nonetheless, I keep alcohol wipes available, since a quick swipe of alcohol removes any offending glue.

Detailed Instructions

⋮ Select two same-sized fabric pieces of matching or contrasting colors.

⋮ Press the fabrics individually.

⋮ Cut a piece of fusible web just slightly smaller than the fabrics.

⋮ Sandwich the fusible web between the fabrics, making sure the wrong sides of both fabrics are next to the adhesive. This gives you two usable sides.

⋮ Beginning in the center, press with an up-and-down motion, following the manufacturer's instructions. Allow the piece to cool.

⋮ Patterns can be traced onto either side of the double fabric piece with pencil and then cut out inside the drawn lines, or pieces can be cut free-hand.

⋮ Pin the elements into position and stitch anywhere and any way desired.

Step 4: Embellish with Colored Pencils

Embellishing is a fairly generic word. It can mean simply sewing on a button or a bead or adding a few extra decorative stitches. This art also includes dabbing on details with markers, paints, crayons, or, ohmygoodnessgracious, colored pencils! Whatever the method, whatever the medium, embellishing is like eating peanuts. It is difficult to stop with one.

To begin, forget all foregone conclusions about embellishment. Try everything. Start simply, though. That is why this book's bodacious appliqué method deals with the use of the basic, easy-to-manage colored pencils added to machine stitched embellishments.

Like every product in America, there are numerous brands and types of colored pencils in the craft shops. You can use any one you choose, but, as usual, some work better than others. Watercolor pencils are water soluble. This means that the marks wash away. There is a method to make their marks semi-permanent, but that requires the application of gel medium over the water color pencil work. Why not opt for a pencil that is more resistant to water?

My preference is waxy, clay-based Prismacolor® Premier colored pencils found in the craft store art department or art supply stores. These pencils require a light touch so that they won't break, but the results are delightful. Very subtle marks can be made, or very strong color can be applied. The marks can be blended with your finger because body heat encourages the wax to sink into the fiber. I always iron the final work. It doesn't seem to make a major difference; it just makes me feel better!

Waxy pencils can be scrubbed out sometimes. That's good news. If wax pencil marks are just rinsed under water, they do not fade away. I suppose if one

seriously wanted to get rid of them, that's when the pencil mark would refuse to budge!

The best news is that colored pencil application can continue after the quilt is finished. If an appliqué needs more detailing after it's sewn or even quilted, all you have to do is find the pencil! The other good news is that, with this book's methods, the pencil work can be done first. If nothing has been cut out at this point, you will work on a square of fabric, which is easier to control than a smaller piece or one with bias edges.

Hand Coloring on Fabric

All quilters, or so it seems, remember a childhood of crayons and paper dolls. Little did we know then that today we would be recalling those glorious experiences while engaged in a similar pastime. Similar, because embellishing fabric with colored pencils is not far removed from coloring pictures with crayons. The difference is that we are not filling in all the color on a line drawing, unless, of course, we choose to do that very thing. These memories and similarities will enable you to feel free to color on your fabric intuitively.

My favorite cottons for hand coloring are the marbled and sponged fabrics that began their existence as solids. They offer beautiful areas that accept shading and contouring without interference of other designs.

Choosing fabric is one of the enjoyable tasks when planning to apply color. You can literally use any fabric and any weight as long as it is conducive to color pencil application.

Sometimes upholstery and drapery fabrics can be too textured to evenly apply color. Having said that, I occasionally find some wonderful textured pieces that work quite well. If you are new to the coloring on fabric technique, start with the easiest fabrics, cottons.

Batiks offer a firm hand and interesting, varied colorations on which to capitalize, especially for wildlife appliqués. For raw-edge techniques, such as Methods One, Two, or Three, batik offers a firm edge when cut. This trait alone is quite often a big reason to use batiks.

Even plain old solid fabric can be effectively used for hand coloring. The best dolphins I've ever done were once a solid piece of gray-blue.

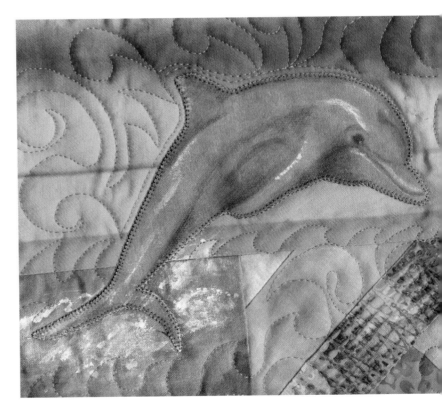

One of my best dolphins.

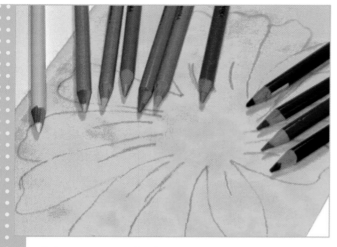

Select a variety of values.

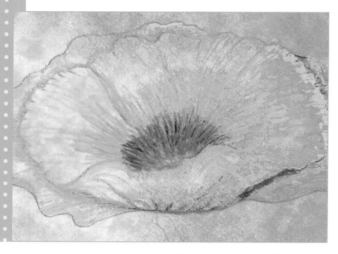

Light, repetitive strokes follow the contour of the appliqué motif.

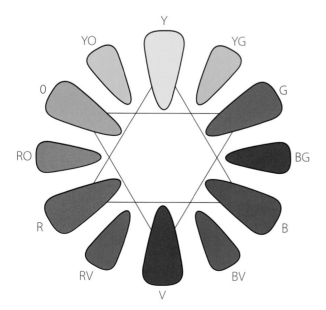

Fabric preparation for hand coloring is simple. You will need some sort of stabilizer on the fabric so that it is easy to color on. Follow the directions given in **Step 3, Choose a Bodacious Applique à la Carte Method,** page 13.

If you are planning to use other appliqué methods, prepare the fabric for hand coloring by ironing a piece of freezer paper to the wrong side of the fabric. Do this by placing the shiny side of the paper onto the wrong side of the fabric. Then press with a dry iron that has a temperature setting to match the fabric content. The freezer paper will stabilize the fabric.

Selecting pencil colors for your project is reminiscent of opening a beautiful new box of crayons as a child. Enjoy the array and then choose a few that go well with the appliqué fabric. Pull out shades that are darker and lighter values than the fabric. These can be the same color or related colors that are adjacent on a color wheel. For instance, if coloring orange flowers, reach for yellows and reds as well as the oranges.

The dark colors must be truly dark and readily seen on the fabric to make your work effective. Consider two or three darks. Try the darkest value of the color you are using, the darkest value of a related color, and the color complement. For instance, when doing a red bird, pull out a dark red such as burgundy, plus dark violet, and the darkest hue of the complementary color, which is green.

Finally, do not hesitate to use other colors as well. Audition them directly on your fabric, in the margins of the drawn appliqué design. Keep your box of pencils at your elbow, and feel free to enjoy additional hues and values. *Just don't overdo the color application so that the colors become muddy.*

Techniques with Colored Pencils

⁘ Begin with a soft touch and light, repetitive strokes. This is the same technique makeup artists use to apply eyebrow pencil.

⁘ Use the side of the pencil as well as the point.

⁘ Keep the pencil sharp with the correct sharpener, usually a hand-held tool, sold alongside the colored pencils.

⁘ Audition the color by stroking on the fabric outside the drawn design.

⁘ Think shape rather than straight lines. Follow the contour of the design such as the curves and waves found in flower petals, bird feathers, and any or all of nature's beautiful products.

⁘ Often, less is more. On the other hand, it's your quilt, so more can be more if you choose!

⁘ Think value by shading areas that need depth. Use a dark value or the color complement.

⁘ Underline with white pencil and then add color atop the white to yield a clearer color change from the fabric's color.

Detail showing areas lightened with white fabric ink.

Using Fabric Markers with Colored Pencils

As you become a hand coloring enthusiast, you will find that fabric markers are good partners with colored pencils. Markers come in a variety of sizes and types of points. The fine-pointed Pigma® pens are useful for any type of stroke, while the various-sized brush end markers easily fill areas. Fabrico® markers with dual tips are also very reliable.

For this book's projects, most of the embellishing is done with colored pencils. There are rare moments, though, when you will need a marker to fill in a very dark area, such as a bird's beak or flower throat.

Occasionally, such as when working on a multifaceted fabric, you will need to lighten, rather than darken, an area. To do this, you can color the area with white colored pencil or white marker, then apply the desired colored pencil on top. Since white markers can be hard to find, white fabric ink applied with a felt dauber is a good alternative. I use Tsukineko® all-purpose white ink.

Relating to Color

All color is relative to its neighbor. If one area stands out, the adjacent area recedes. The recessive area is shaded darker than the one moving forward. To move to the forefront, an area can be lightened so that it will wave proudly. Its neighbor will move backward because it is darker. Relax, have fun, and do not over-analyze this. You had no questions when you did this as a child!

Consider where you want to direct your viewer's attention. Usually, when we look at a quilt our eyes seek a focal point. On a quilt, the appliqué itself can be that focal point. Yet, within the same appliqué there can be a focal point, or area of emphasis, which gives the appliqué a special beauty.

You, the artist, possess the freedom to decide if you want a focus within an appliqué and where you want it. This emphasis might be one prominent flower petal with several colors showing or with textures imparting importance. It could be the throat of a flower, wherein lie the mysteries of the flower's creation, its sepals and stamens and dark colorations. Within that area could be swirls of water or a lurking insect. Ask yourself, "What if...," and proceed with reckless abandon, remembering that this dark flower throat can be very dramatic.

"So, how much color should I apply?" you wonder.

The answer is as much or as little as you want. Consider the question asked in this book's introduction: What did you see in your mind's eye when you began this process? If you saw simplicity, the answer is equally simple. Use the least amount of coloration needed to fulfill that mental image. If, instead, you visualized a very dramatic, large, complex flower with interwoven designs, textures, and colors, then you would most likely add a great variety of hues and values. This is when more is more, and you opt for an "ohmyword!" stunning impact.

At this point, you may look at your appliqué and consider it complete. It may be just perfect as is. Consider, however, that more fun awaits you in the form of stitch embellishment. You have already gone through the decision process of shading and highlighting; now, you can further emphasize and texturize your appliqué by switching chairs and moving to your sewing machine. It's your choice. Bodacious appliqués à la Carte are complete only when the appliqué queen says so!

Add shading that contours with the shape of the design.

Fill in details in the center of the flower.

Decide if the appliqué's details will benefit from stitch embellishment. Partial stitching shows the difference.

Hand Coloring Appliqués

1. Tape your appliqué design to a light box (or window). Place the interfaced fabric directly on the drawing, right side of fabric facing upward. Secure with masking tape.

2. Trace the outside lines of the design with either a #2 pencil or a fine- to medium-point permanent fabric marker that does not feather (bleed ink into areas you do not wish to color). (*Hint:* Try the marker in the margin of the fabric.) These hard lines are easy to see and can be cut away later. If you are tracing on a dark piece of fabric, try a light colored pencil or a white water-soluble marker. If your fabric is so dark that the light box does not help, switch to Method Two, the jigsaw puzzle method, and use the freezer-paper pattern as the outside line guide.

3. Trace the interior contour lines of the design with a medium- or light-value colored pencil that can be seen fairly easily. For this step, use the sharp pointed end of the colored pencil, not the side. Draw any needed details, such as the vein in the middle of a flower petal or the shape of a bird's wing. Do not use the hard edged marker or #2 pencil described above inside the piece because the line produced will leap out visually against the softer shades of the applied colors.

4. Now for the real fun! Remove the fabric from the light desk and work on your table. Give your creative spirit free reign and work intuitively. Look at the design. Determine which areas should be shaded or highlighted. For instance, where a flower petal lies under another, the underlying area will naturally be shadowed by the top petal and should be darker. If a flower petal is dancing in the sun, highlight it with a very light value. Leaf veins have both dark and light sides, offering opportunity for great texture.

Step 5: Embellish with Thread

Threads, Beautiful Threads

Embellishing with machine stitches has taken off with the development of incredible new threads.

Twenty years ago, there were limitations to the fibers, weights, and colors of threads found in the stores. Today, the sky is the limit. Just as we quilters have fabrics stashed everywhere possible, we also have numerous drawers overflowing with threads of all sorts:

- silky-looking cottons of assorted weights and plies, which fill areas beautifully

- rayons with sheen and new strength to endure embroidery designs

- amazingly pliable monofilaments that have unlimited possibilities

- shiny, enticing polyesters usable in a variety of stitching

- shimmering metallics, iridescents, and holographics for glitzy projects

- threads with colors that "evolve" in sunlight

- variegated, hand-dyed creations to warm the cockles of your heart

- threads that go bump in the night or at least glow in the dark!

And every one of these can be used as an embellishment.

Selecting threads is just as much a picnic as is purchasing fabrics. However, rather than sampling all of the above, begin with a thread that is simple to use and will enhance your appliqué in the way you envisioned—start out with cottons or polyesters. Decide whether you want the shine of polyester or the flatter,

Select threads by pulling strands over the fabric.

Stitch embellishment adds texture and beauty to this iris.

matte look of cotton. Both of these thread types play a predominant role in this book's samples.

To choose the thread colors for your appliqué, remember that the appearance of a wound spool of thread against the fabric is different than one thread laid out against the fabric. Unwind the prospective threads and lay them across the appliqué singly, or loop them into a small "puddle." This is a more accurate preview of their effect. This test will help particularly in determining if a thread is too close to the appliqué's color to use.

Your stitch embellishing can be made very effective by using three values of the major color. Choose threads just as you selected colored pencils. For example, if you are creating an orange lily, consider the fabric color as your medium value and select thread hues that are lighter *and* darker oranges.

Add a very dark value thread for the finishing touch. The darkest thread is used in smaller quantities but yields dramatic results. Beware of using your darkest thread in these hues as an outline! Also, do not waste time using thread that is too close in color to its neighbors. Instead, take the cue from your colored pencil shading colors and stitch contoured shadings.

After you have experimented with these easier-to-manage threads, then you will definitely want to progress to using metallic and thicker threads. Since I have never met a thread I did not like, I will only warn you that buying thread is every bit as addictive as buying fabric!

There are many reasons to add beautiful thread embellishment to appliqué. The texture alone gives significant depth and beauty. Even minimal stitching adds great impact. Stitching can add more color, add small details, and even replace quilting in some instances. Some quilters admit that they use thread embellishing to rescue them from disasters such as spots or tears on their quilts.

Your Sewing Machine at Its Best

Just as any worthwhile effort requires prep time, there are preliminaries that lead the way to effective stitching.

First and foremost, clean and oil your machine. Machine manufacturers include a small brush in the tool kit, and that is the greatest prevention of machine problems. Regularly—and by this I mean every six hours of actual sewing, not once every three years—remove the face plate and brush away all dust, lint, and thread particles from every place you can reach. If oil is included, use it in the bobbin race area.

If you are unsure as to the care and feeding of your machine, visit your local dealer and ask. Dealers are usually happy to know that their customers want to know how to maintain their machines.

Needle Me

As our sewing machines have changed and improved, so have machine needles. Variations in type and size give us the opportunity to get the best from our threads. Be willing to invest in various needles so that you will get prime results. Generally, for decorative stitching, use the smallest size and sharpest point needle that works for you and does not break or shred your thread.

My experience is that "sharp" rather than "universal" points work best, particularly on batiks. Most of the time a size 70 sharp needle works well with cotton and synthetic threads. This size needle is able to penetrate the appliqué layers, produces a moderately sized hole, and does not strain the thread. Size 75 is good too, though sometimes difficult to find. It is also labeled as an embroidery needle.

With thinner fabrics, a size 70 needle can prove effective because it limits the "play" on the thread.

This is especially true when using monofilament. *If the thread begins to shred or break, I immediately change to a new needle, and if the problem persists, I change to a new, larger size needle.*

The appliqué queen who enjoys stitching on denim will soon discover the reason for jeans needles and sizes 80 and 90. The finer needles do not hold up when sewing such thick fibers. Sometimes students think they should use an 80 or 90 size needle for all their quilting simply because the needles are larger and do not readily break under stress. My suggestion is to try the smaller size, then graduate to the larger size only if necessary. Remember, the difference in the needle size is echoed by the size of the hole in the fabric. Appliqué queens do not have large holes throughout their quilts (unless this is part of your design, of course).

One needle ranks among my favorites—the topstitch needle is my all-time friend when I am switching thread types on a project. Because it has a deeper scarf, it does not tend to shred the thread. Best of all, it serves metallic thread very well. *When stitching with metallic thread, it is imperative to use either a Metafil, metallic, or topstitch needle.* Any other needle will make you hate metallic thread! I sometimes like to stitch with two threads, treating them as a single thread when threading the machine. *The topstitch needle gives me a balanced stitch with the two threads.*

Bobbin Along

Many students today wisely ask, "What sort of thread do I put in the bobbin?" It is a credit to all of us that we have learned to consider this variable. Even the manufacturers are trying to answer this question with a simple tool—prewound bobbins. These bobbins are especially welcomed by the home embroiderer.

Do not let the many bobbin options cause confusion. If you are using cotton or polyester threads, the easiest answer to the question of bobbin thread, at least at the outset, is to use the same thread on top and in the bobbin. *When your top thread is a monofilament, a metallic, and perhaps even a rayon, you will not want the same thread in the bobbin.* For these specialty threads, which have specific needle requirements, you will get better results by using a cotton or polyester thread in the bobbin. You can still match its color to the top thread, if desired.

On very rare occasions, you may encounter a stitcher who tells you that she uses monofilament as a bobbin thread. That may work for her, but your life will be easier if you stick to using monofilament as a top thread. There may come a time when you want to use monofilament in the bobbin; at that time, make sure you use a pliable thread such as cotton or polyester on top. When you meet the moment that you want to put monofilament in the bobbin, wind the bobbin only half full. *Too much monofilament wound tightly on a bobbin can actually squeeze and distort the bobbin.*

Why is thread type an issue? Understand that threads contain a certain amount of elasticity to do their jobs. They also have to be strong, and some are stronger than others. Rayon has the least resiliency under pressure. What this means to you is that if you have a super strong thread, such as monofilament or some of the Mylar® threads, you should balance them with a thread that has good elasticity, such as cotton or polyester. Do not overthink this, but be ready to change the bobbin thread if it is not giving good results. *If problems appear when using a metallic on top and a cotton in the bobbin, try changing to a polyester in the bobbin.*

Tension Anyone?

Tension is an essential, not for you (Relax! Have fun!), but for your machine.

Basically, for a thread to make a good stitch, it must have the correct amount of tension, or pull, placed on it by the machine. When you thread the machine, you pull the thread through tension discs at the top of the machine. The tension setting determines the pressure on the thread after you lower the presser foot. It is important that you understand that the presser foot should be raised when you are threading the machine. Otherwise, the thread is not dropped between the discs and will not stitch effectively.

To balance the tension, you change the number on the tension knob. Raising the number tightens the tension. Most of the time, you will find yourself lowering the tension to accommodate variations in threads. *Monofilament, metallic, and polyester threads are surprisingly strong, so be prepared to lower the tension by a couple of numbers when using them.*

Checking and changing the tension is something you do *before* you begin sewing directly on your project. This means you need a test piece on which to try out the stitching. Ideally, the test piece is comprised of the same fabrics as the final project, or, you can test stitch tension on the margin of your project. Save yourself later woes and develop the habit of testing threads and tension. Decide which threads and needles to use, then give them a trial run. Do enough stitching so that when you pull the

Tension Test Tip

Label samples of various tension settings/thread combinations and use them as a reference to save time on future projects using similar fabrics.

fabric out of the machine, you can tell if it has any puckering. If the fabric is pulling up, that is puckering, and the solution is to lower the top thread tension. Raise the presser foot, lower the tension, then test this new setting.

The end result you are seeking is a beautiful stitch resulting from balanced tension. Look at the stitching. Turn the piece over and examine the back. If the thread is lying across the fabric and is barely held in place by loops from the top thread, the top tension must be tightened. Raise the number and stitch another test.

In rare cases, the bobbin tension must also be altered. Years ago, when everyone sewed with the same thread and had few choices for their bobbin threads, machine repairmen threatened us with bodily harm if we dared to change that itty bitty screw on the bobbin case. Now we know better. Sometimes, that little screw needs a minute change to loosen or tighten the tension on the bobbin thread. Today, many folks who like to use all sorts of threads opt to purchase a second bobbin case to which they make changes. They reserve the primary bobbin case for projects using typical "normal" threads.

Remember, you are seeking balance so that your work does not pucker. The top tension is the first key. Changing the bobbin thread is the second. The correct needle size for your thread and fabric is third.

Machine Options

We live in an amazing sewing world. Manufacturers are diligently producing more and more tools so they can claim our attention and our unending allegiance. Fortunately, this gives us a multitude of choices. At times, it also adds a dilemma or two with so many machine option decisions to make.

This unsatisfactory result gave me the Bodacious Appliqué idea.

Feet First

Sewing machine companies continue to offer new feet so that we can get desired results. Many machine feet are now closed- or open-toed.

The open-toed **appliqué foot** facilitates appliqué stitching because it allows us to see the exact stitch placement.

For free-motion stitching, a **quilting foot** *(originally called the darning foot)* with a spring attached allows the quilter to drop the machine's feed dogs and move the fabric herself, thus determining the size of the stitch by the movement of the cloth.

The **edge foot** assists in sewing appliqués and stems an equal distance from the edge of the motif; this foot requires the machine's ability to move the needle position to the desired stitch placement.

The **quarter-inch foot,** with or without a side bar, keeps our pieced seam allowances one-quarter inch wide (if we use it correctly).

The **walking foot,** always an essential for machine-guided quilting and for adding trims and bulky items, can be purchased open- or closed-toed. It moves both the bottom and top fabrics together as one unit so that wrinkles and puckers are avoided. One company has even made it possible to change its walking foot from closed to open with the twist of a screw.

Just as quilters have grown accustomed to using the quarter-inch foot, appliqué artists are equally fond of the concept of open-toe machine feet. The open-toe format first appeared on the appliqué foot and dramatically increased visibility. Very quickly, and for the same reason, the darning foot, also called the quilting foot, lost a part of itself and became open-toed. Not to be left out, some of the walking feet gained the option of being open-toed, and quilters danced all the way to the store to purchase them. Remember, these are optional, but they are downright nice to have. As a quilter and appliqué artist, you will never regret purchasing these tools. You will also be delighted that you made the purchase sooner rather than later! We do this for enjoyment, don't we?

Another machine option concerns thread stands. As more and more threads entered our sewing world, they showed up on a variety of spools. Not surprisingly, the thread was even wound on the spools in different ways. This is only worth notice because the way the thread is wound on the spool may affect your machine's stitches.

Rather than trying to assimilate details about cross-wound vs. parallel-wound spooling, you simply need to know you have the option of sewing with the spool placed on a horizontal or a vertical spindle. Many machines come with both spindles. You can purchase a separate thread stand, which enables the thread to be pulled above the spool before it is threaded in the machine. Elaborate multi-thread holders are being manufactured, but I still love the simple, inexpensive one-spool spindle that instantly makes friends with all threads. To make it simple, if the thread is not coming off the spool easily in its existing position, change the spool's position.

Hoops

Before materials such as fusible interfacings and water-soluble stabilizers were available to the home seamstress, we were taught to hoop fabrics that we wanted to embellish. The process worked well then, and it still works.

For our purposes, when using a hoop for stitch-embellished appliqués, the fusible interfacing already fused to the appliqué fabric is the stabilizer. A second stabilizer can be added if your stitching becomes extremely dense. In that instance, pin water-soluble paper to the fabric without unhooping the project.

To use a hoop, loosen the outer ring and place it so that it lies flat on a table. Select the size that encompasses most of the appliqué design. The outer appliqué edges are not stitched at this time. Place the appliqué over the hoop, with the right side of the appliqué facing upward. Press the inner ring of the hoop over the appliqué into the outer ring. This places the fabric next to the machine's feed dogs rather than having space below the fabric. Lower the feed dogs, grasp the hoop, and free-motion stitch.

Hint: Hooped fabric should be taut, but not stretched a great deal. *If it is pulled too tightly in the hoop, new problems occur as the fabric relaxes to its natural position after the hoop is removed—the stitching doesn't have enough space, so it tends to pull up.*

Fewer embellishment stitches are needed on the edges of pieces within the hoop because they will eventually be edge-stitched to a background. If I feel that embellishment is needed at the edges, I do those simultaneously with the edge stitching when applying the appliqué to its background. The good news is that your appliqués are yours, and you can do as much or as little stitching as you desire! Sometimes, less is more; but at other times, more is more! You get to choose!

Free-Motion Embellishing

Use these steps to embellish your appliqué before sewing it to its background. The examples given are for flowers, but the process is the same for other subjects.

❖ Pin water-soluble stabilizer to the back of the appliqué.

❖ Lower the feed dogs on your machine.

❖ Bring the bobbin thread to the top of the fabric. Begin sewing with a securing stitch, which, rather than a knot, is a sequence of very small stitches. After 6-8 tiny stitches, proceed to your customary free-motion rhythm and stitch length. Snip away the thread tails.

❖ If you prefer no initial tiny stitches, begin with your preferred stitch length and leave the thread tails intact on the top. Upon completion with that thread, pull both threads to the back and tie a very secure small knot.

Easy Does It

Sew thread embellishments at a moderate, not fast, speed. A great deal of heat on the thread is produced during sewing, and slowing your motor speed is a good practice. This is most important when using metallic threads.

If you find yourself stitching so densely that puckers are appearing, either add another stabilizer behind the appliqué or place the appliqué into a hoop. See the puckering photo on page 29 for an example of what to avoid.

Effective stitch embellishment can be minimal, such as shown in the orange lily, or it can be intense, such as in the gold gazania.

❖ Start stitching with a medium-value thread. For flowers, the medium-colored area is usually the midsection of each petal. Think shape, and stitch lines that follow the contours of the petals. Stitch back and forth in short strokes as opposed to single lines. Straight lines are rarely needed. Stitching should be continuous, even when in short strokes.

❖ Travel to the next petal by stitching through the throat of the flower. *Even bodacious stitching can be minimal, especially when used in combination with hand coloring.* Often, the dark pencil shaded areas can stand alone, requiring little additional stitching.

❖ Switch to the lighter-value thread and stitch areas to be highlighted, such as petals in the forefront and areas where the sun reflects.

❖ Stamens and seeds are stitched with a free-motion zigzag resembling a satin stitch. This stitching can be made continuous by returning to the flower throat and moving to the next petal.

❖ Stitch with the darkest thread last. It will add the most drama but does not require huge amounts. Use it to heighten shaded areas.

❖ Give the piece a final press.

Use your imagination when stitching. This is a fuchsia version of the gazania pattern in the WINDBLOWN WISHES quilt.

The dark thread colors add drama to this gaillardia, especially in the center.

Step 6: Audition Fabric Backgrounds and Stitch

Amazing, isn't it, that the time it takes to read and digest the previous chapters is about the same amount of time it will take to develop an appliqué!

At this point, having followed the directions, you are embracing a bodacious, hand-colored, machine-stitched appliqué. It is either still on that square of fabric with the interfacing on the back, or it was cut out as listed in the steps of Method One, page 14. If you have not yet cut it out, do so now, using your best fabric scissors.

It is time to return to your fabric stash to select background fabrics. Follow your instincts and pull out a few pieces that are distinctly different, such as a dark, a light, a medium, a large print, and a small print. If possible, audition your appliqué on the background pinned to a design wall. Stand several feet away from the wall. Looking at a vertical piece from a distance gives a better view and perspective than looking at your project as it lies flat on a table.

If you cannot make a quick decision, get out your digital camera and take pictures. The advantage of using a digital camera is that you can compare the photos in the camera without printing them. You can also download them to your computer and then study them in larger format, or with all the photos spread side by side on the computer screen.

After you have chosen your background fabric, cut it to size, but allow a tad extra. For example, if the block is to be 12½" (12" finished), cut it 13". Just remember later on to trim the block to its correct measurement.

Sunflower, from the POSTER GIRLS OF SPRING quilt, is one piece, hand colored, then stitched. Note that each petal is blanket-stitched to add depth and differentiation.

Audition various background fabrics and stem fabrics for your appliqué.

Add depth and definition to your one-fabric appliqué by stitching into the piece and following petal lines, which have been colored in.

Place the appliqués on the selected background and spend a few moments trying out various angles and positions. For a more artistic feel, consider placing objects off center. Ask yourself which placement makes the piece more interesting and more dynamic.

If your project requires additional elements, such as stems and leaves on a flower, *audition those along with the focus piece.* Try out stem placement by curving it in various ways. Place the stem's raw edge under the flower and pin it into position. Realize that stems give the viewer's eye a direction, so consider what you want that stem to do in order to enhance the piece.

Eventually, you will find the perfect placement for everything, so pin all of the à la Carte pieces in place.

Meanwhile, back at your chair, the sewing machine awaits. Everything you learned about stitch embellishment in **Step 5, Embellish with Thread,** page 25, comes into play again. You will need the correct needle, the proper foot, and your choice of threads and stitches. The machine foot of choice is an open-toe appliqué foot.

Select your favorite stitches for the appliqués and let your machine show its stuff. Before fusible products, it seemed that everyone stitched appliqués with a satin stitch. Currently, we see more variety. Stitchers have found the adaptability of functional stitches such as the hem stitch, zigzag, and the utility stretch stitch, which mimics a blanket stitch. The blanket stitch has long been my favorite. Unless there is a good reason to use something else, I call upon it often, always varying the width and length to suit the piece.

To stitch the appliqués, begin with those elements that will appear as if behind other items. For a flower, for example, the first element to stitch is the stem, with its raw edge lying under the flower. If leaves extend under the stem, those should be securely pinned under the stem to be stitched with the stem or stitched down before the stem (in the correct position, of course). The flower itself is usually the last piece stitched.

Occasionally, a floral design requires a long stem. Pinning a stem and maintaining a graceful curve can be challenging. Rather than tearing out spastic curves later, you might *begin by hand basting the stem into position with a long stitch through the center of the stem.* Begin with the knot on the front so that it will be easily removed when the stitching is complete.

Some machines have an edge foot, which makes topstitching stems easier than with any other foot. The edge of this foot nestles next to the stem, and the needle position is moved to place the stitches where you want them. By keeping the foot's edge right next to the stem, you get a surprisingly almost perfect line of stitching. This does not even require magnifying glasses! *Remember to test this stitch on a trial piece and make any necessary tension adjustments before the final stitching.* Another stitching option is to apply the stem with a decorative stitch. The CERULEAN WILDFLOWER project, pages 39–41, uses this idea. When the stitching is complete, give your project a final press. Then, put on your appliqué queen crown and call for applause.

RIGHT: *Detail of the CERULEAN WILDFLOWER.*

Step 7: Use the à la Carte Approach

As you peruse the pattern pages that follow, hopefully a design will call out, saying, "Make me, make me!"

Rather than duplicate my work in this book, consider this your invitation to creative freedom. Embrace your own mental image of the design and follow your instincts, combining any background idea with various design possibilities.

Therein is the beauty of the à la Carte approach. You begin with any number of motifs, or appliqué pieces, complete them to your liking while using any bodacious appliqué method, and then position them anywhere you want to create your own project. By auditioning fabrics as you go, you can assure yourself of having enough contrast to show off your work.

Making Bias Flower Stems

Some of the à la Carte designs incorporate flower stems. My favorite type of stem is made from a bias strip so that it can be shaped or curved into pleasing lines. A tool called a bias bar makes this a simple task. Cut the width of the bias strip twice the item's desired finished width plus ½". For example, to make a finished half-inch wide stem, cut a strip that is 1½" wide. Cut the stem's length about an inch longer than the pattern shows to give yourself some placement wiggle room.

To sew the stem, fold the bias strip in half along the strip length, wrong sides together. Stitch this together lengthwise using a quarter-inch seam. Trim the seam to ⅛". Insert a bias bar into the sewn tube and roll the seam to the center of the bar. Press the stem very well, seam to one side. Continue to push the bar through the stem, rolling the seam to the center, and ironing.

After removing the bar, allow the stem to curl in the way you wish, then press again. In this manner, stems can be shaped into curves and circles with relative ease and pressed before they are pinned to their permanent positions. The raw edges of the ends are tucked under their adjoining appliqués or disappear into border seams. For example, notice the stems in the POSTER GIRLS OF SPRING quilt, page 61.

Adding Accent Strips

In some projects, such as MEADOWLARK, page 42, accent strips are used. You can easily add these any time you are seeking extra highlights around a section. The strips may simply border a focus area and extend ¼"–½" into the focus area. To add to its fun, DC'S GARDEN OF GLEE, page 84, has a ½" accent strip.

Decide how wide an accent strip you want and cut a piece of fabric twice the desired width plus ½" for seam allowance. Cut the length equal to the side of the focus area to which it will be sewn. Fold the accent strip, wrong sides together, in half lengthwise. Align the strip's raw edge to the raw edge of the background fabric and baste through all three layers. Borders or sashing are sewn on top of the strip. Press the seam so that the accent strips lie flat. They will stay in place very nicely and do their job, which is to highlight an area or to provide a separation between two colors.

Throw in a Few Beads, Why Not???

Many of today's appliqué queens add beads to their appliqués. Beading is another addictive form of embellishment. If you choose to add beads, it is up to you *when* you add them. By using fusible interfacing, you can add beads in the interiors of these appliqués before applying them to the background and the beads will be secure. Another beader might apply the beads after the appliqué is securely sewn onto its

background. Others wait until the quilt top is together. I could go on with this, but you get the idea.

The best news is that you get to add beads your way! If you scrutinize the photographs, you will spot beads in the TROPICAL ENCOUNTER project detail shown on this page. Given more time, some beads will probably find their ways into MEADOW-LARK, page 42, and OUT OF THE SWAMP, page 54! You see, Dear Reader, beaded quilts can become neverending stories!

Choices! *À la Carte Projects*

(Or, Design Your Own Bodacious Appliqué Quilt)

CERULEAN WILDFLOWER

20" x 20"

Simple and effective, this flower is one fabric, à la Method One, that of creating depth on one fabric. Because the fabric color is so deep, the center is colored white first, then the lime is penciled over. Just for fun, a machine decorative stitch is used to fasten down the stem. If you choose to add such stitching, be prepared to lower the top machine tension and pin a tearaway or water-soluble stabilizer behind the background. Run a small trial sample to test the tension.

The design in the border is drawn with markers and colored pencils, and then later quilted alongside the lines. To draw these designs, stabilize the border fabric with freezer paper pressed shiny side to the back of the fabric. Free-motion floral designs finish the quilting.

Yardage Requirements and Cutting

Background: 1 fat quarter (18" x 22")
    cut one 15½" x 20½" piece

Appliqués: 10" fabric piece for the flower
    4" x 6" piece for leaf

Stem: 1½" x 14" bias strip

Single Border: ⅙ yard
    cut selvedge to selvedge, 5" x 20½"

Sash between border and appliqué block:
    1½" x 20½" strip

OPPOSITE: *CERULEAN WILDFLOWER*

RIGHT: *PURPLE WATERLEAF, 26" x 20". PURPLE WATERLEAF varies from the CERULEAN WILDFLOWER project by using two borders. The quilt is machine appliquéd and free-motion machine quilted.*

*M*EADOWLARK, *24" x 26", made by the author.*

MEADOWLARK

24" x 26"

MEADOWLARK is a progressive design because elements are easily added as the piece develops. Each motif uses one fabric piece, following Method One. Machine decorative stitches are sewn on the leaves *before* they are cut out. The gold edge on the violet leaf became part of the design because the accent color seemed appropriate to tie in the gold stitching on the leaf. That gold edge is slipped under the leaf and fused. You can create this design as it is shown and go on to add additional leaves and curls as well. The honey-colored bird is free-motion stitched with metallic thread. The quilting begins by echoing all of the elements in a continuous sweep, and then breaks into free motion.

Yardage Requirements and Cutting

Background: ⅔ yard
  cut one 22" x 24" piece

Borders: ⅙ yard
  cut one 2½" x 22"; cut one 2½" x 26"

Accent Strips: cut one 1" x 22" and
  one 1" x 24"

RIGHT: *HONEY AND SAGE, 26" x 29". A variation of MEADOWLARK, HONEY AND SAGE is machine appliqué enhanced with trapunto, free-motion and machine-guided quilting, and hand beading.*

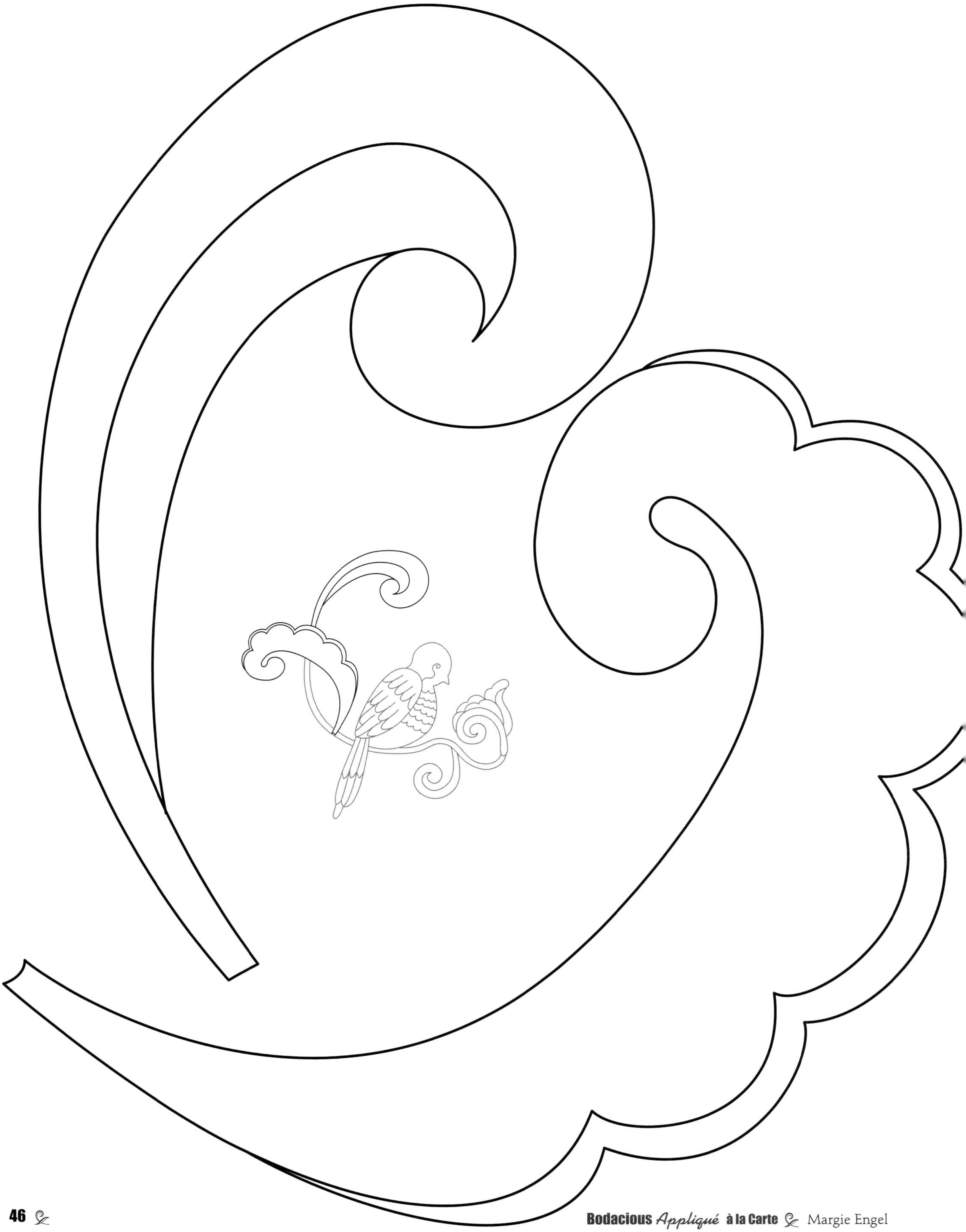

BEAUREGARD, 40" x 42", made by the author.

BEAUREGARD

40" x 42"

Stunning and vociferous, this magnificent macaw only looks difficult. Following Method One, his body is a large piece of red fabric and a small blue insert. The beak and feet are hand colored using both markers and pencils. On the beak, use a dark marker first, then highlight it with white on the top section. Color his feet the same way. Draw in as many feathers as you wish, then free-motion stitch them, using different values of thread to get the desired effect. The leaves and flowers are also made using Method One. Free-motion quilting creates a jungle vine and leaf design.

Yardage Requirements and Cutting

Background fabric: 1 yard – cut 33" x 42" (or whatever width your fabric is)

Macaw Body: 20" fabric piece

Macaw Tail: 20" fabric piece

Leaves behind Bird: 18" fabric pieces

Jungle Leaves: 12–15" fabric pieces

Flowers: 5" fabric pieces

Borders: ¼ yard – cut two 4½" x 42" strips

Stitching Hint: Because the leaves next to the macaw are a linen fabric, which ravels and precludes raw-edge appliqué, satin stitching their edges was necessary. *To minimize raveling, I placed clear water-soluble stabilizer atop the leaves before stitching.* This greatly improved the stitch quality, especially at the points. The clear stabilizer is easily pulled off, so complete immersing is not even necessary.

Enlarge leaf patterns 200%

Enlarge leaf patterns 200%

Enlarge bird pattern 200%

Enlarge bird pattern 200%

Out of the Swamp, 28" x 29", made by the author.

OUT OF THE SWAMP

28" x 29"

All of the flowers—jack-in-the-pulpit, yellow skunk cabbage and marsh belle—are made using Method One. Each is one fabric, hand colored and machine stitched before it is cut out. Jack's leaves are one piece of fabric, embellished, cut out, then sewn before adding the flower head. Assemble the quilt in two sections, treating the left side with the two flowers and sashes as one part, and the jack-in-the-pulpit block with its side sashes as the other section. Consult the cutting diagram for clarification.

```
+------------------------------------------------+
|              28½" x 3½"                         |
+------+------------------+-----+-------+---------+
|      | 9½" x 2½"        |     |       |         |
|      +------------------|     |       |         |
| 3½"  | 9½" x 8½"        | 2½" | 9½" x | 2½"  3½"|
|  x   |                  |  x  | 18½"  |  x    x  |
| 26½" +------------------| 18½"|       | 18½" 26½"|
|      | 9½" x 2½"        |     |       |         |
|      +------------------+-----+-------+         |
|      |                  |                       |
|      | 9½" x 14½"       |  13½" x 3½"           |
|      |                  +----------------------+|
|      |                  |  13½" x 5½"           |
+------+------------------+-----------------------+
```

Quilt cutting diagram

Yardage Requirements and Cutting

(Fabric amounts assume that one fabric each is used for background, sashes and borders. If you combine fabrics, you will need lesser amounts.)

Backgrounds for appliqués: 5/8 yard
cut one 9½" x 8½"; one 9½" x 14½";
one 9½" x 18½"

Sashes: ½ yard – cut two 9½" x 2½"
(above and below the belle flower);
two 2½" x 18½" (the sides of jack's block);
one 13½" x 3½" sash (the bottom of jack's
block)

First Borders: ¼ yard – cut 3½" x 26½"
(for the left of the quilt);
cut 13½" x 5½" (the border under the
bottom sash sewn to jack's block)

Top and Right Borders: ¼ yard
cut 26½" x 3½" (right side final border);
cut 28½" x 3½" (top border)

Appliqué Fabrics: assorted 12" pieces for jack,
jack's leaves and skunk cabbage; 7" piece
for marsh belle and skunk cabbage leaves

Stems: 1¼" wide bias strips, sewn from
various fabrics

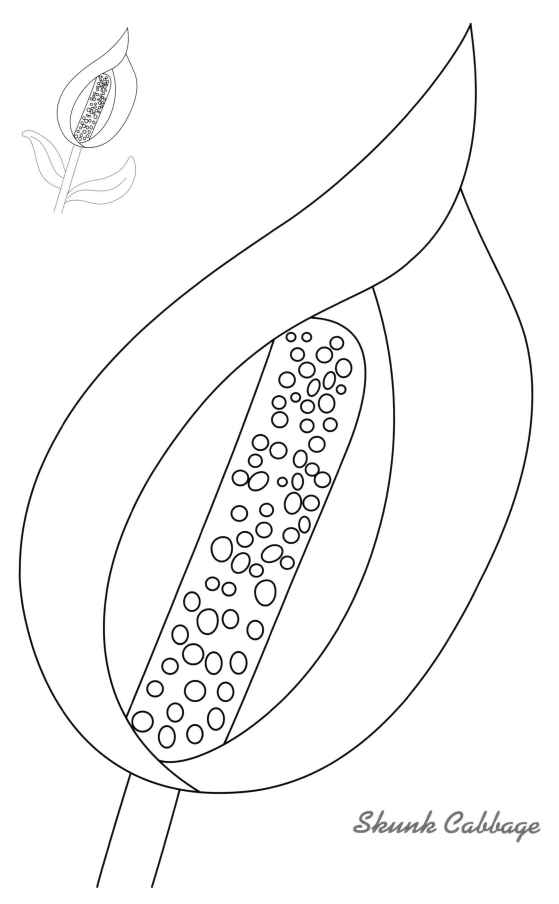

Skunk Cabbage

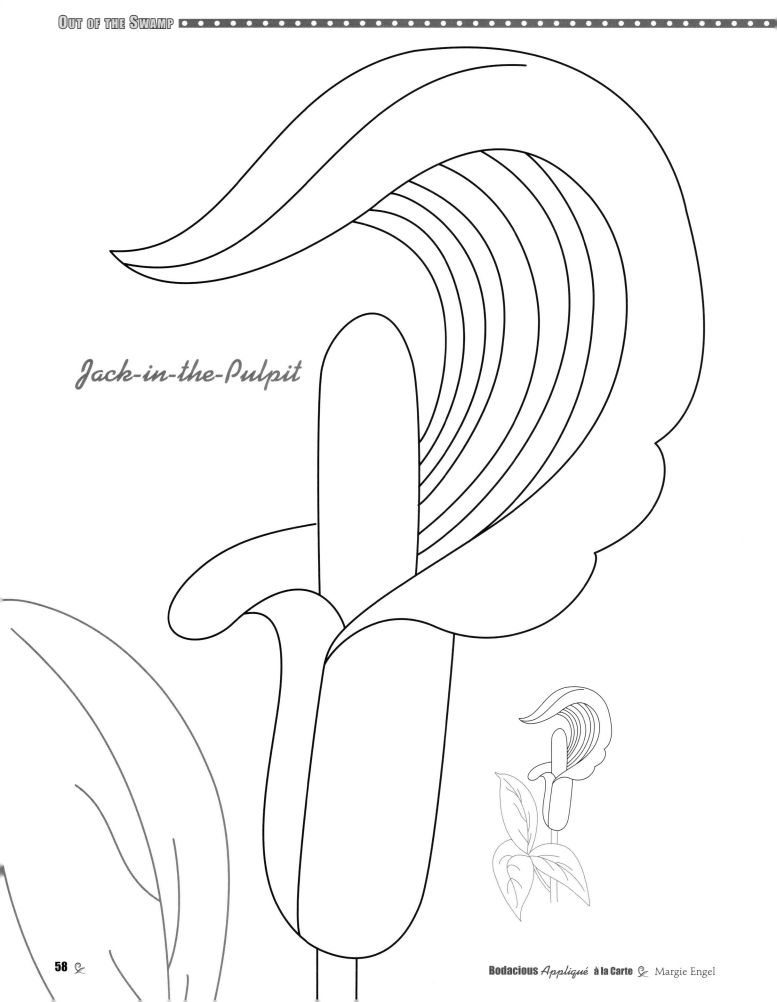

Jack-in-the-Pulpit

Marsh Belle

POSTER GIRLS OF SPRING, 48" x 38", made by the author.

Poster Girls of Spring

48" x 38"

Welcome to the poster girls' party, where the flowers can all be created using Method One and only one piece of fabric, should you so choose. In the photograph, the iris was actually created using Method Two and three fabrics. Suit yourself, as one fabric can be as effective when hand colored. Using either method, each flower is hand colored and stitch embellished. These may appear involved, but this is an illusion created by using several different threads and colors, including variegated combinations in the quilting.

To assemble the quilt, follow the diagram for cutting and assembly. Each flower is framed by sewing top and bottom sashes, then adding the side sashes. Consult the photograph for color placement.

Yardage Requirements

Frames: ¼ yard each of two fabrics

Sashes and Borders: ¾ yard

Stems: 1¾" wide bias strips of various fabrics cut in various lengths

Appliqués: 12" fabric piece for the hibiscus, 10" fabric pieces for the other flowers; small scraps for the leaves

Cutting Measurements

Frames: Cut, selvedge to selvedge, five strips from each fabric, each 1½" wide.

From the first fabric *(green in the example)* 1½" strips, cut the following frames: four 10½", two 12½", two 14½", and four 16½".

From the second fabric *(orange in the example)* 1½" strips, cut the following frames: four 10½", two 12½", four 14½", and two 16½".

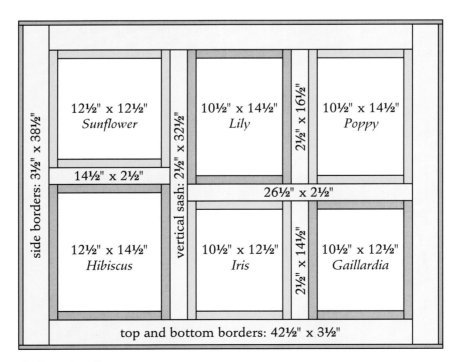

Quilt cutting diagram

Sunflower

Lily

Bodacious *Appliqué* **à la Carte** Margie Engel

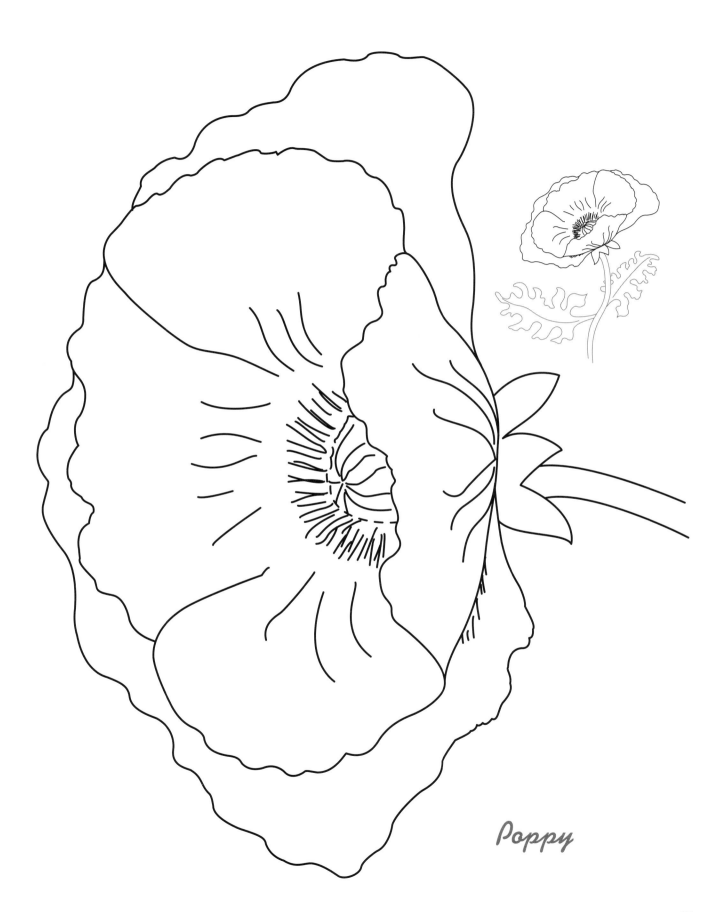

Poppy

Enlarge hibiscus pattern 200%

Hibiscus

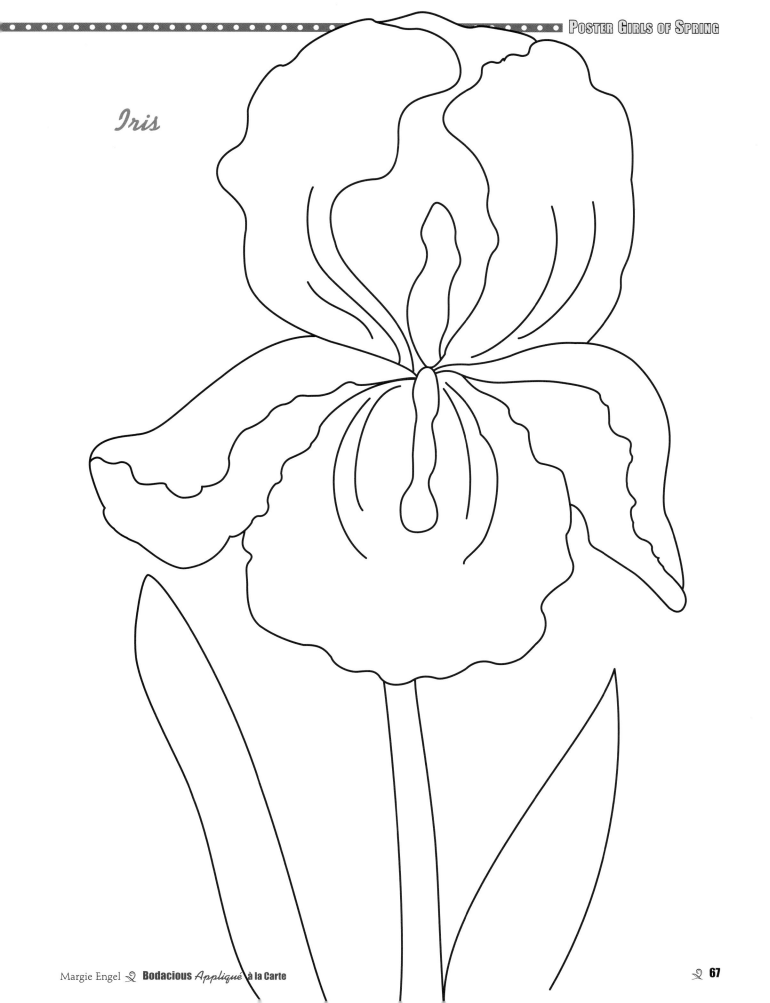

Iris

Gaillardia

Leaves

Tropical Encounter, 28" x 38", made by the author.

TROPICAL ENCOUNTER

28" x 38"

Following Method Two the flowers are comprised of two parts, the colored portion and the base. The geckos are each one piece of fabric, hand colored and machine embellished before they are cut out. The background batik has a vine design that was loosely followed for the free-motion quilting. As an "accidental beader," I found this to be a wonderful project for beading.

Yardage Requirements and Cutting

Background Fabric: 1⅛ yard *because it is a directional fabric* – cut a 22" x 38" piece. Non-directional fabric requires only ⅔ yard.

Side borders: 1⅛ yard – cut two 3½" x 38" strips (can be pieced from less yardage)

Stems: 1½" x 16" bias strips

Appliques: 8 assorted 10" fabric pieces

Enlarge flower patterns 200%

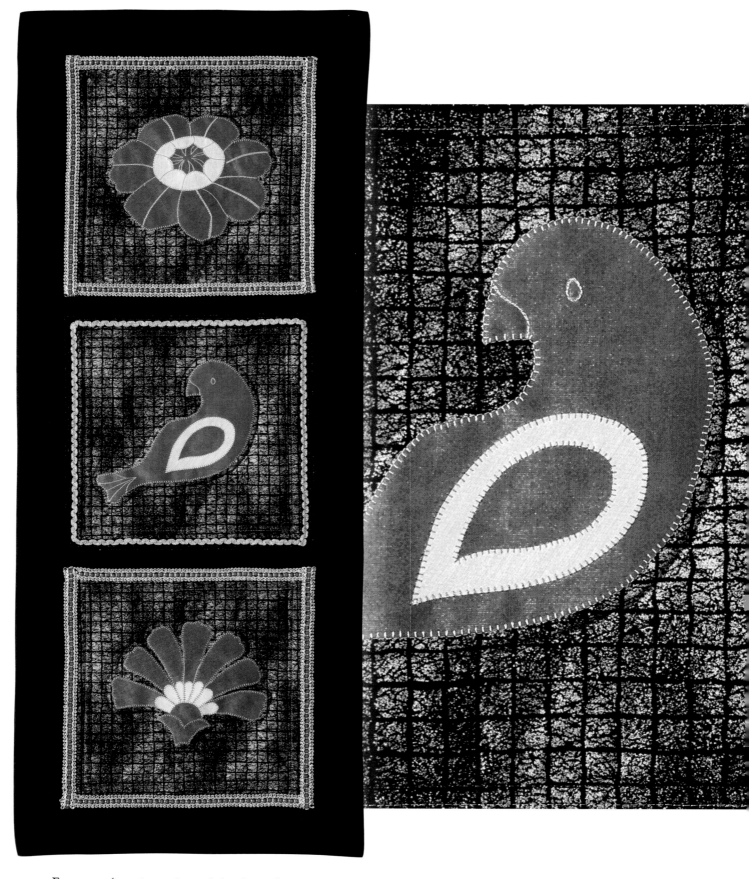

ELEGANTÉ, 15" x 38", made by the author.

ELEGANTÉ

14" x 38"

This formal arrangement cried out to be made of iridescent cotton-nylon fabric and metallic gold thread. Because the ruby cotton lamé fabric has a tendency to ravel, I chose to back the motifs with Steam-a-Seam 2® fusible web to prevent ragged edges.

Fuse the motifs to the background, then stitch embellish. Little embellishment is needed, but if you choose to do a great deal more, pin a tearaway or water-soluble paper stabilizer behind the background.

Refer to the photograph to assemble the quilt. The two horizontal sashes as well as the top and bottom borders are sewn to the quilt before the final addition of the side borders. The side borders are added, and the gold trim is added after the quilt is sewn. For the quilting, the appliqués are initially echo-quilted with dark monofilament. Straight-stitch quilting with metallic threads follows.

Hints for adding trims: Allow the trim to lie naturally and pin or baste it into position without pulling it taut. To stitch by machine, use a walking foot. Monofilament can be useful as a top thread, but loosen the top tension, generally decreasing it by two numbers. Extensive raveling on cut edges can be tamed by applying clear nail polish or a stitch sealant. Pretest these and allow them to dry before stitching the trim.

Yardage Requirements and Cutting

Background Fabric: ⅓ yard
    cut three 10½" squares

Sashes and Borders: ⅓ yard
    cut four 2½" x 10½" strips for sashes and top and bottom borders
    cut two 2½" x 38½" strips for side borders

Appliqué fabrics: 8" fabric squares

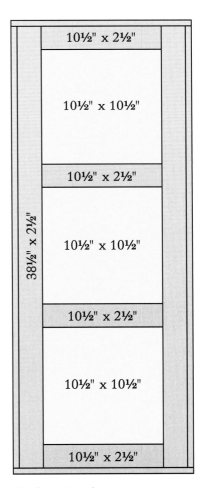

Quilt cutting diagram

WINDBLOWN WISHES, 24" x 31", made by the author.

WINDBLOWN WISHES

24" x 31"

A weed to some, a salad to others, the dandelion is a visual delight when it's winged seeds soar into the wind. On this piece, the wispy seeds rise and scatter wherever the artist wishes! The wisps come into being as machine quilting and are stitched with white and metallic threads.

The dandelions and their leaves are double-sided (Method Four), using fused pieces of green and gold fabrics. Each leaf is stitched into position through the middle (vein), allowing the edges to float freely. The dandelion flowers and buds are free-motion topstitched into position.

The top flowers, gazanias, follow Method One using one gold piece of fabric with the maroon sections colored in, then enhanced with stitching. Consult the photograph and the diagram for placement and assembly. Note that the side borders are sewn prior to the top and bottom borders.

Yardage Requirements and Cutting

Background Fabric: ½ yard
cut one 13½" x 12½" piece and one 13½" x 9½" piece.

Vertical side sashes that adjoin appliqué blocks: ¼ yard
cut one 4½" x 12½" and one 4½" x 9½"

Middle Sash and Borders: ¾ yard
cut as follows:
middle sash, 17½" x 2½"
side borders, 4" x 23½"
top border, 24½" x 3"
bottom border, 24½" x 5"

Gazania Appliqué: 10" fabric square

Gazania Stems: cut 1" x 14" bias strip

Dandelion Stems: cut ¾" x 14" bias strip

Dandelions and Leaves: use a variety of fabric scraps

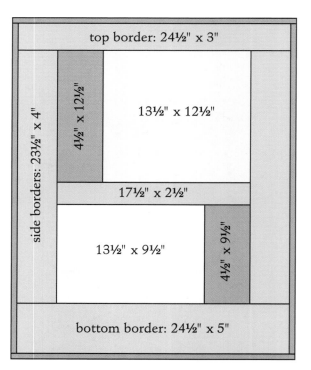

Quilt cutting diagram

Quilting motif

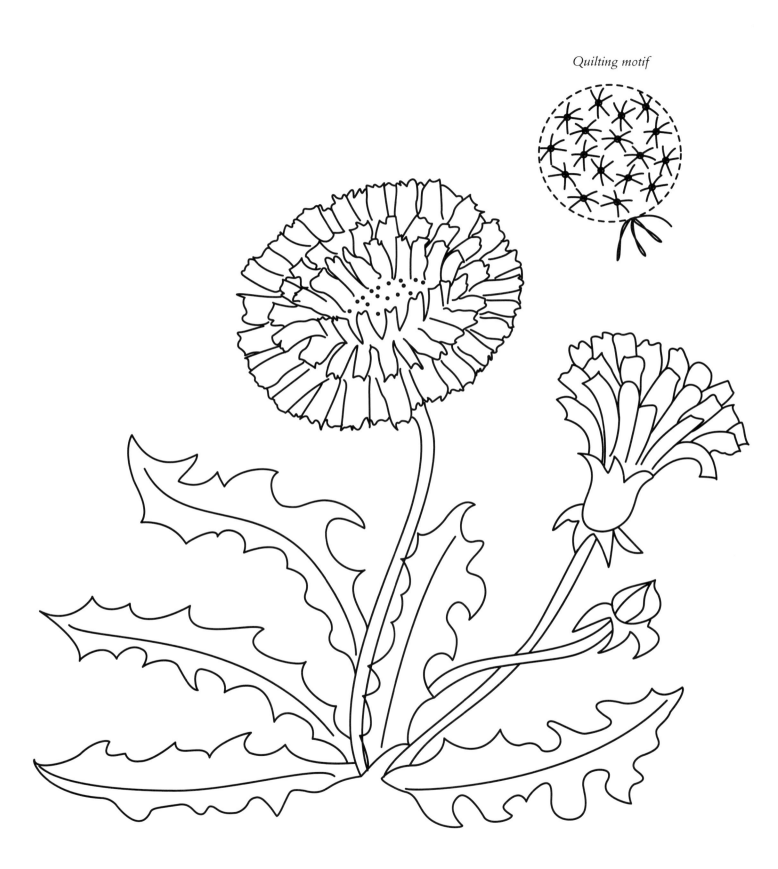

LEFT: *Quilting motif detail for WINDBLOWN WISHES.*

DC's GARDEN OF GLEE, 31" x 23", made by the author.

DC's Garden of Glee

31" x 23"

Dear Cat (or Darn Cat!) loves catnip, as will you when creating your own banquet of fabrics and machine stitches by creatively using several stitches, decorative or functional. This no-rules project provides unlimited freedom and the fun of playing with your machine.

If you want to play with DC and recreate his garden, I suggest you follow these construction steps:

❖ Go directly to your fabric collection and pull out your favorite wild fabrics. Include a variety of greens for stems, leaves, and catnip. Cut three 15" bias strips of varying widths from 1" to 1¼". Stitch these into stems, which you can cut into lengths as desired.

❖ Prepare double-sided greens (Method Four), using contrasting fabrics on each side. Cut out wiggly catnip/clover pieces either freehand or draw them directly onto the fabric with a pencil, then cut them out.

❖ Using fusible web (Method Three), create the flower pieces, their leaves, and the cat. Hand color the cat's features with markers, pencils, or ink.

❖ Cut the background fabric 26" x 18". With all the prepared elements on the work surface, dive in with reckless abandon and arrange the elements of your piece!

❖ Pin or hand baste the stems, then stitch them into position.

❖ Press the fused pieces into position, then stitch them into position, using a variety of stitches and threads.

❖ Randomly place the catnip and clover in front of the cat, then stitch/embellish them through the center of each unit.

❖ Audition borders and add any number that pleases you. The side borders for my work are cut 18" x 3" and are sewn before the top and bottom borders. The top and bottom borders are cut 31" x 3".

❖ Accent strips are optional. Consult **"Adding Accent Strips" in Step 7,** page 36, **Use the à la Carte Approach.**

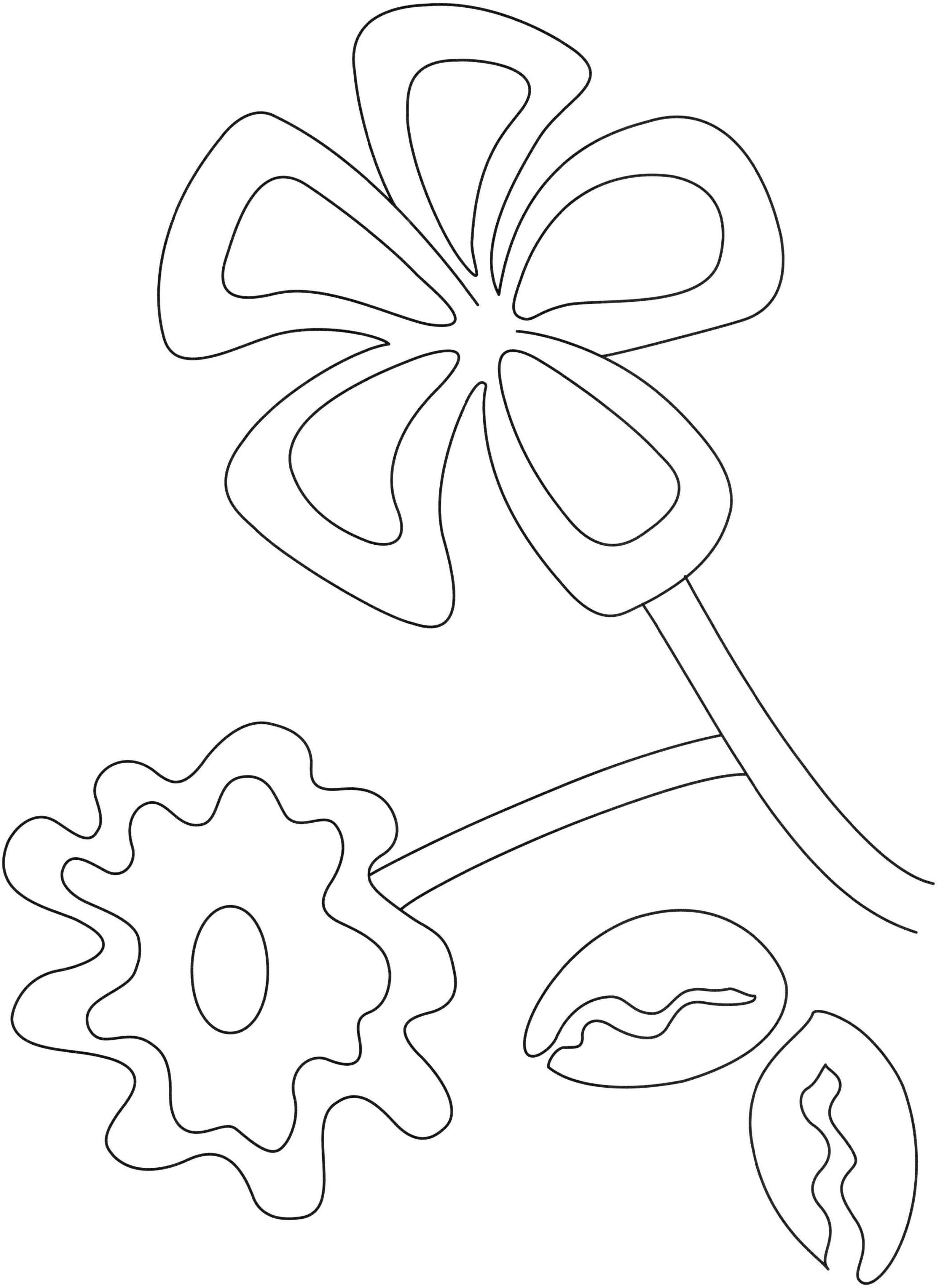

Inspiration! *A Gallery of Quilts*

FUNKY FUSIBLES, 47" x 23", made by the author.
FUNKY FUSIBLES is all fused, machine appliquéd, and machine quilted.

Moonstones, 27" x 28", made by the author.
Moonstones uses the appliqué motifs from Eleganté as machine quilting designs, which are heavily beaded.

IRIS AT DAWN, 31" x 32", made by the author.
Strip-pieced blocks provide the background for the large iris.
Quilt is machine appliquéd and free-motion machine quilted.

FLORAL ILLUSIONS is 34 x 42. Machine quilted and machine appliqued, made by the author. The flowers on the upper left and lower right strips of fabric were painted with white all-purpose ink.

Resources!

Always support your local quilt shop when you can. Ask if they carry the product you are seeking. They may be able to order it for you if they don't.

Amann USA

www.ackermannna.com

Isacord® and Yenmet® threads

HTCW Inc.

www. HTCWproducts.net

Form Flex 100% cotton stabilizer

American and Efird, Inc.

www.amerfird.com/mettler.htm

Mettler® threads

Sakura Color Products of America

www.sakuraofamerica.com

Pigma®Micron® acid-free pens

Sanford L.P.

www.prismacolor.com

Prismacolor® Premier pencils

Sulky of America

www.sulky.com

Paper Solvy™ (water-soluble stabilizer), threads

Superior Threads

www.superiorthreads.com

Wide variety of threads

Tsukineko, Inc.

www.tsukineko.com

All purpose inks, applicators, and Fabrico® Markers

The Warm Company

www.warmcompany.com

Paper-backed fusible Steam-a-Seam® products
Warm and Natural® batting

YLI Corporation

www.ylicorp.com

Wide variety of threads

About the Author! *Margie Engel*

Although she lives on a Florida beach, Margie Engel likes nothing better than spending the day inside—in her sewing studio. Taught to sew at the age of five by her mother, she was stitching appliqués to doll house linens with embroidery floss by age six.

In their first year of marriage, Margie's husband, John, gave her a sewing machine. She happily sewed decorative stitches that produced girly dresses for their daughters and embellished their household linens. Although quilts were not part of her textile heritage, it was the color and design possibilities and the desire for a Christmas wall quilt that led her to try out quilting. An artist was born! Today, she holds numerous quilt award ribbons.

Margie is founder and president of EduQuilters, a group of volunteers who take "The Kids Quilt Project" into schools, organizations, and summer camps. For this work she has received several community service awards, including the Jefferson Award for Public Service. She wrote *Kids Quilt Projects In and Out of the Classroom* to help others introduce quilting to children.

Margie teaches high school sewing teachers on land, leads retreats aboard cruise ships, and heads symposiums for quilt guilds. Sharing her creativity through *Bodacious Appliqué à la Carte* is a natural step in her life. You may reach Margie at: www.EngelQuilts.com.

Other AQS Books!

This is only a small selection of the books available from the American Quilter's Society. AQS books are known worldwide for timely topics, clear writing, beautiful color photos, and accurate illustrations and patterns. The following books are available from your local bookseller, quilt shop, or public library.

#7778	us$26.95
#7772	us$26.95
#7600	us$26.95
#7608	us$26.95
#7604	us$24.95
#7602	us$26.95
#7605	us$24.95
#7494	us$21.95
#7607	us$26.95

Look for these books nationally.
Call or **Visit** our Web site at

1-800-626-5420
www.AmericanQuilter.com